IN THE
WORKPLACE

Construction

CATH SENKER

Evans

Contents

Working in Construction

A job in construction could allow you to work on all kinds of building projects. You might be helping to construct a brand-new housing estate, a state-of-the-art sports stadium or an impressive bridge. You could even be restoring historic buildings to their former glory.

The construction industry is hugely important for people and the economy, providing much-needed housing, offices and public buildings. The way it operates is significant for the environment too – the construction of environmentally friendly buildings can help to reduce carbon dioxide emissions.

A WORLD OF OPPORTUNITY

A variety of businesses are involved in the construction industry. You might work for an international company engaged in giant construction projects worldwide or a small family-run business maintaining local homes. You could be a self-employed craft worker, for example a cabinet-maker, taking on jobs for builders or individuals.

HANDY HINT
Today the construction industry has to follow environmental standards laid down by government to make buildings more sustainable. If you keep up to date with new sustainable building methods, you'll be an asset to the industry.

A rare example of a female construction worker. A tiny proportion of people working in the construction trades are women, although more work in the professional and technical sectors.

A technician carries out a site inspection. Large numbers of skilled people are required to plan, organise and check construction jobs.

Many different types of jobs are available, including professional, technical and hands-on work. You could be designing an arts centre or using specialist skills as a CAD operative, bricklayer or carpenter.

In construction, you can start at any level and work your way up to a senior job or gain enough experience to set up your own business. Although most people in the construction industry are men, there are opportunities for women too. For example, in the USA in 2007, 1 per cent of employed women worked in natural resources, construction and maintenance occupations – that's around 680,000 women.

FINDING A JOB

With a good general education, including GCSEs in English and maths, you can start in a trade as an apprentice. This allows you to earn while you learn. You will work most of the week and study part-time at college to gain qualifications.

LOCATION AND HOURS

Your job could be local or anywhere in the country. Construction work can take you abroad too. In this sector, you should be prepared to travel, and at times you may have to live away from home for a while. As regards working hours, generally you'll work a normal working week, but it is likely that you will have to do overtime as well. Sometimes you'll need to work long hours to meet deadlines.

RIGHT FOR THE JOB?

Large construction projects bring together teams of workers, so you need to be able to work well with other people. If you'd prefer to work alone, you can be self-employed and take on small jobs. Many construction tasks require strength and stamina, so you should be fit and healthy. You'll often be working outdoors or in half-finished buildings, in all weathers and in difficult conditions. A head for heights is useful for many jobs, such as scaffolding and roofing. You'll have to be aware of health and safety issues – building sites can be dangerous places.

Preparing for Construction

At the start of a construction job, the labourers demolish the old structures and prepare for the new building. First on the scene are the outdoor workers, including the demolition operatives, plant operatives and scaffolders.

Y ou can train for these types of employment on the job – a good way is to do an apprenticeship. You'll be given extensive training in first aid and health and safety because you may come into contact with hazardous materials, and the work itself can be risky.

DEMOLITION OPERATIVE

Much construction work takes place on brownfield sites – locations with buildings that were used previously but are no longer needed. To prepare the construction site, demolition operatives dismantle the unwanted structures.

Smashing down buildings may sound easy, but it's a skilled job. First, you erect fences around the site. Then you remove any reusable fixtures and fittings. After that, you take away doors and windows. Once hand demolition is completed, experienced operatives use specialist oxy-fuel cutting equipment to demolish the structure safely. They may even need to use explosives. It's a dramatic moment when the structure finally comes tumbling down!

TO WORK IN CONSTRUCTION, YOU WILL NEED

●

physical fitness

●

good manual skills

●

an awareness of safety issues

Demolition work requires the skilled use of large machinery, such as this crane.

KNOCK-OUT JOB

For this job, you should be capable of working at heights and in all weather conditions. You'll require good manual skills and should be able to carry and use heavy equipment. Bear in mind that you'll be working in dusty, dirty and noisy conditions. You'll have to wear a range of protective gear, including goggles, a helmet and ear protectors. Sometimes you'll require breathing equipment too.

Here, the Kaiser Hospital in Hawaii is demolished using controlled explosions. The building collapses amid billowing dust.

FINDING A JOB

You can start out as a general construction operative (labourer) to gain experience. You'll do basic tasks such as moving building materials and helping to lay drains, as well as operating equipment such as cement mixers.

HANDY HINT

Outdoor construction jobs can be exciting and are great if you want to avoid a 9 to 5 office existence. But it's worth knowing that construction workers are prone to ill-health because of the hard physical work they do. Common health issues include back pain from lifting and carrying heavy objects; skin and breathing problems from dust and toxic substances used in construction; and hearing difficulties owing to noise levels and vibration.

PLANT OPERATIVE

If you like the idea of driving and operating massive diggers and dump trucks on a construction site, this job could be for you. As a plant operative, you operate all kinds of vehicles, including bulldozers, excavators, diggers and cranes. One day you might be using an enormous 360-degree excavator to shift huge quantities of soil and rock. Another day you could be using a static tower crane to lift heavy building materials into position. You might also operate machines required for the building process, such as concrete mixers and rollers for flattening out the work area.

As well as working on site, you'll be responsible for driving these monster vehicles to and from building sites – a skilled job in itself. You'll also need to carry out regular safety checks on the plant.

IN THE CAB

Working conditions on the construction site may be dusty, muddy, noisy, cold or hot. You'll mostly be working in the cab of the vehicle, sometimes at a great height, using levers and switches to control the machine.

TO BECOME A PLANT OPERATIVE, YOU WILL NEED

●

some knowledge of construction machinery

●

the ability to concentrate hard

●

the ability to work safely and responsibly

The best way to train to work with bulldozers and other heavy equipment is to take an apprenticeship.

Martin – *plant operative*

Today, large machines are computer controlled. This driver uses a computer system to guide most of the crane's actions.

'I've been driving and operating plant for 18 years. When I left school, I wasn't sure what to do. I tried mechanics and then decided on the building trade. I had a go at stonemasonry and then became interested in machines. I found employment on a building site and learnt to operate plant on the job. Nowadays you need some training before you start operating the machines.

'I work a nine-hour day. I'm qualified to operate many different kinds of plant. On a typical day I could be using a forward-tipping dump truck, a 360-degree excavator or a telescopic forklift. These machines can move vast quantities of material – the excavator can shift a load of up to 30 tonnes! I do various kinds of jobs. I might be laying down pipes underground or preparing roads for tarmac.

'Operating plant is great on a cold and wet day because I'm nice and dry in the cab! It's satisfying using large machines, doing a big job on a big scale. At the end of the day, you can see the results of your work. It can be a bit lonely though. The other site workers are in a team, while I'm in my own little world in the cab.

'If you're interested in being a plant operator, there are several options. In some jobs you might just be doing demolition, while in another you might only be laying pipes. It's best to come into the industry and try it out.'

**TO BECOME A
SCAFFOLDER, YOU
WILL NEED**

•

to be an excellent team worker

•

*an excellent sense of balance
and a head for heights*

•

physical fitness

UP ON THE SCAFFOLDING

Got a head for heights? Scaffolders put up scaffolding for new construction projects and to enable maintenance work on existing structures. You could be erecting scaffolding for housing, a bridge, stands in a sports stadium or even a film set. You'll usually work outdoors although there are some indoor jobs.

Creating scaffolding involves joining tubes together to form a framework and fixing scaffold boards on to it. You'll need to be able to take measurements accurately and use a variety of hand tools, such as spanners to fix the tubes together and a spirit level to check the boards are horizontal.

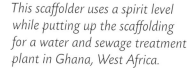

This scaffolder uses a spirit level while putting up the scaffolding for a water and sewage treatment plant in Ghana, West Africa.

Safety is crucial. You have to keep yourself and your workmates safe while working at great heights, and ensure that the scaffolding is secure to avoid causing any harm to passers-by. This job requires a high level of concentration. It's tough, physical work. You'll need to be fit and strong to climb up and down the ladders while carrying heavy equipment.

Tim – scaffolder

'I've been working as a scaffolder for ten years. When I started out I didn't know anything about the job. I began by doing basic tasks, such as fetching scaffolding and carrying it up the ladders. I worked my way up and now I'm a supervisor.

'I work for a medium-sized scaffolding company and we're subcontracted to work on different sites. The jobs vary – we might do three or four small jobs in a day, or we could be working on a big project for a while. I work an eight-day hour day, but I have to travel to work, and the job could be two hours' drive away.

'Many people have a go at scaffolding work and give up after just a couple of weeks. It's not for the faint-hearted. The job is very physical. There could be 12 tonnes of gear to move into position and you might have to triple shift it to get it there. That's moving the gear three times, so it's like shifting 36 tonnes of material! Building sites are noisy and dirty. When you take down scaffolding, it's covered in sand and cement from the construction work, so you go home absolutely filthy at the end of the day.

'As a scaffolder you get fit, and you become so used to carrying heavy materials that you barely notice it. It's a steady job, with good prospects of progressing to supervisory levels. It's become a respected profession too. Other workers on site appreciate that you're doing a tough job.'

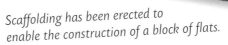

Scaffolding has been erected to enable the construction of a block of flats.

Putting Up Buildings

After the foundations are laid, a host of craftspeople help to put up the new building: bricklayers construct the walls, carpenters build the wooden structures and roofers create the roof. Other specialists play their part too, such as floor layers, glaziers and tilers.

As for the jobs in chapter 1, you can train while you're working or take an apprenticeship, which allows you to work and to study part-time to gain qualifications.

LAY IT ON WITH A TROWEL

Bricklayers build and maintain the outside and inside walls of all kinds of buildings. As a bricklayer, you use hammers to cut bricks or stones to the right shape. You spread mortar with a trowel, and then lay the bricks accurately in position.

Stonemasons specialise in working with stone. There are two main types. Banker masons use hand and power tools to carve stones for new buildings and to restore old buildings. Fixers build stone walls or repair stonework. Some stonemasons design monuments and memorials.

BUILDING SKILLS

Bricklayers and stonemasons mostly work outdoors in all weathers, and the conditions can be dirty and dusty. You'll often have to stand or kneel for long periods, and the work can be repetitive. You'll need to be fit to lift heavy materials. It's important to be able to follow plans accurately and to have a good eye to check the walls are perfectly straight.

MAIN TASKS – STONEMASON

●

following design instructions

●

carving stone

●

using tools to create a finish on the stone

●

building stone walls

●

repairing damaged stonework

FINDING A JOB
There are no particular qualifications required to start as a bricklayer or stonemason, but employers usually take on people who have some experience. It is useful to work as a labourer on a building site first. Once in a job, you may be able to train as a bricklayer or stonemason.

Bricklayers have to work fast but accurately. This bricklayer checks that the wall he is constructing is perfectly straight.

Bricklaying is a tough job physically. This bricklayer has to bend down for long periods while building up the wall.

Dennis – bricklayer

'I've been a bricklayer for about 20 years. First I went to college and took a two-year bricklaying course. Then I went to work for a friend who was a contractor, and I received first-class training.

'Bricklayers usually work an eight-hour day. It's very demanding on the body because you're constantly lifting bricks, bending and twisting. I found that the job suited me though. Once I'd gained experience, I became self-employed.

'When you work for yourself, you can either do price work and be paid according to the number of bricks you lay, or you can work for an hourly rate. If you're experienced and can lay around 600 bricks a day, it can be better to go for price work. You can do your measure – lay all your bricks for the day – and go home. The downside is that you can't work when the weather is really bad, and sometimes you have to make a month's pay last for six weeks.

'After ten years working for myself, I took a job as a supervisor. Now I have a guaranteed regular wage.

'If you're considering working as a bricklayer, it's worth taking a college course to get qualified. When you're looking for work, check that you'll be trained by an expert tradesperson so that you can progress in the industry.'

WORKING WITH WOOD

Carpenters and joiners make and repair wooden structures, such as staircases, doors, floorboards and window frames. Bench joiners work in workshops making parts; site carpenters fit the parts; and shopfitters specialise in giving stores a makeover. Formwork carpenters make moulds (called formwork) for concrete structures, such as the pillars in multi-storey car parks. The wooden structures hold the freshly placed concrete in place until it has hardened. As well as working on new buildings, carpenters help to improve existing buildings, working on extensions or repairing woodwork.

Naturally, to be a carpenter you'll have a love of wood! You'll be comfortable handling power tools such as sanders and jigsaws. You'll need first-rate manual skills for using good old-fashioned hammers and chisels too. A knowledge of maths is vital for taking accurate measurements and calculating angles; sometimes you'll need to work out how to fit wood into awkward spaces. Wood is heavy, so you'll need to be strong to shift the materials.

Working conditions can be challenging. You'll frequently be working on a dirty building site in all weathers, often in an uncomfortable position. Carpenters have to bend, kneel, crouch or stand for a long time. You'll often need to wear protective gear, such as goggles and ear protectors. The workshop environment can be unpleasant too – the air is full of wood dust.

BE YOUR OWN BOSS

You can gain experience in different types of carpentry and progress to become a supervisor. Alternatively, with a few years' experience under your belt, you could become self-employed.

TO BECOME A CARPENTER, YOU WILL NEED

●

good manual skills

●

to be able to follow plans

●

physical fitness

This carpenter uses a machine called a router with a diamond-shaped device clamped to it. It allows him to cut a diamond-shaped inlay in the wood.

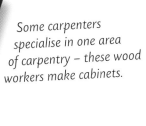

Some carpenters specialise in one area of carpentry – these wood workers make cabinets.

Stuart – carpenter

'I've been a carpenter for about eight years. I started out doing a two-year apprenticeship – I worked four days a week and went to college one day a week. Afterwards I worked for a company for a year and then became self-employed.

'I mostly work in a team doing loft conversions. We put steel beams in the joists, insulate them and then put the floor down. Then we build the dormer window, first creating the side walls and joists and then applying the new roof. We put in the internal walls and put up plasterboard inside. Then we cut the stairwell and put in the stairs. Sometimes I lay a wooden floor.

'The work can be tough. I'm on my knees a lot of the time, often in tight spaces, so it can be uncomfortable and tiring. It's a brilliant trade to learn though. Carpentry can be well paid – it's usually better if you're self-employed.

'If you're thinking about a job in carpentry, decide whether you'd rather work in a workshop as a joiner or as an on-site carpenter. I'd advise you to study as much as you can, which will give you better job opportunities.'

ON THE ROOF

Once the structure of a building is in place, it requires a roof. This is where the roofers come in. Roofers construct and repair roofs on all types of buildings, including houses, offices, public buildings and shopping centres.

There are two main kinds of roof – flat and pitched (sloped). You can work on both kinds or focus on one type. There are different kinds of roofing materials too, including tiles, slate, asphalt, felt and sheet materials. Again, you can train to use various materials or decide to focus on one type. You'll use different tools depending on the materials you're working with.

SLATE, TILES AND BITUMINOUS ROOFS

Roof slaters and tilers lay new tiles and slates or replace broken ones. You'll learn to lay the slates or tiles in rows and to cut the end and corner pieces to fit. To create bituminous roofing, you cut and measure areas of felt and place them in layers on top of one another. You lay hot bitumen on to each layer of felt to damp-proof it. Some roofers may also damp-proof masonry and concrete walls and floors.

A roofer lays shingles on a building, the final part of a roofing job. The shingles form a protective layer that keeps out rainwater.

MAIN TASKS – ROOFER

laying new roofs

repairing existing roofs

installing weatherproof shields

installing roof sheeting or cladding

waterproofing masonry

SPECIAL ROOFS

You could work on some extraordinary types of roofs. In a conservation job, you might repair the roof of a stately home or palace. You might even learn the old-fashioned craft of thatching. Today, a small but increasing number of buildings have 'green' roofs. After installing a waterproof lining, you place layers of soil on top so that plants and grass can be grown there.

ON TOP OF THE WORLD

Clearly, to be a roofer you'll need to be happy to climb ladders and scaffolding, often carrying tools and materials, and to work at heights. In this potentially dangerous occupation, you often need to wear a harness for safety. This is a physically demanding job, especially in hot, cold or windy weather. The higher up you are, the harsher the conditions can be. It's worth knowing that some roofing materials, such as roof sheeting, are hard to handle.

As this is an outdoor job, you'll work during daylight hours, and there may be overtime. You'll need to move from site to site for work, and may have to spend some time away from home.

WHERE WILL I BE?
In all the outdoor jobs, you can work your way up to technical, supervisory or managerial levels within a company. With several years' experience, you can choose to set up your own business.

This roofer is helping to construct the roof of a new London Underground tunnel – a huge roofing job.

TO BECOME A GLAZIER, YOU WILL NEED

●

good manual skills

●

to be able to measure and calculate accurately

●

a strong awareness of safety

EXPERTS IN THE HOUSE

How about specialising as a floor layer, glazier or tiler? This sort of work offers a lot of job satisfaction but it can be challenging. Although perhaps not as physically demanding as being a roofer or bricklayer, you will need to carry heavy materials and sometimes work in difficult conditions.

ON THE FLOOR

Floor layers lay different kinds of flooring, such as carpets, vinyl, tiles or timber. You could be putting down hard-wearing rubber flooring in a factory, stone tiles in a kitchen, or carpets in a private home. You may choose to become expert in one type of flooring.

As a floor layer, first you measure the area and draw up a plan or diagram. You also measure the flooring material. It's crucial to be able to make accurate plans and follow them carefully. The calculations can be quite complicated – floors do not always have straight edges, especially in older properties, but the floor must have no gaps. Then you prepare the surface to ensure it is clean, level and dry. You cut the flooring material to the exact measurements, which requires good co-ordination.

IN THE WINDOW

Glaziers work with glass and other window materials, such as plastic glass substitutes. They install and repair windows in homes and for businesses. For this job, you need to be able to calculate accurately and work carefully because glass is fragile and can be dangerous. Awareness of health and safety is crucial.

A flooring expert uses an electric jigsaw to lay a wooden parquet floor in the living room of a house.

WHERE WILL I BE?

It's possible to enter all the building jobs in this chapter as a trainee or apprentice and work your way up. With experience, you can move into a supervisory position, become self-employed or set up your own business.

This job can involve work at all hours – glass may get broken at any time of day or night. You could be called out in an emergency to repair the glass window of a shop front that has been smashed in the middle of the night.

ON THE TILES

Tilers tile the walls and floors of all kinds of buildings to create durable, easy-to-clean surfaces. You could be tiling in homes, supermarkets or hospitals. You prepare the surface, spread adhesive and lay the tiles. Some tilers undertake artistic work, creating decorative tiling. As well as having first-class manual skills to lay the tiles accurately, it's useful to have some design and colour sense for advising customers.

These glaziers use a suction clamp to position a sheet of glass in a new shopping and leisure centre. Glaziers often have to work at heights.

Inside Jobs

Once the building has been constructed, a variety of craft workers arrive to carry out the interior jobs. They include electricians, plumbers, plasterers, painters and decorators. A sensible way of training for these kinds of jobs is to become an apprentice.

BRIGHT SPARKS – ELECTRICIANS

Electricians install and check wiring systems in all types of buildings. As an electrician, you could be working in homes, factories or out on the streets, fixing lighting and traffic systems.

This is a highly skilled job. You need to be adept with your hands and able to use a variety of tools, such as drills and screwdrivers. You'll need to be highly safety conscious to work with electricity and to know the regulations governing the installation of electrical systems. It's important to be capable in maths, technology and science – particularly physics – to understand the principles of electricity and to work out wiring diagrams.

It's helpful to have an interest in new technology too. New installation methods are continually being developed. Many local governments and businesses are trying to reduce their electricity use and are investing in new ways to light, heat and ventilate their buildings. As an electrical apprentice, you can learn how to work with solar, wind and geothermal energy systems. Increasingly, electricians are expected to be proficient in ICT, for example, to work on computer-controlled building management systems. If you keep up with the latest developments, you will be greatly in demand!

An electrician tests for live wires while installing a new domestic electricity meter.

TO BECOME AN ELECTRICIAN, YOU WILL NEED
●
normal colour vision to differentiate between different-coloured wires
●
physical fitness
●
good communication skills

This electrician wires a ceiling rose in a house. Electricians need to be good at problem solving to identify faults in wiring systems.

ON THE JOB
The conditions vary depending on where you work. You could be in a warm home updating the wiring system or up a ladder on a cold day repairing a street lamp. In general, the job involves a lot of bending, stretching and working in cramped situations. You may also have to work at heights. Sometimes you'll work alone, although on a big project you'll be part of a team.

MAIN TASKS – ELECTRICIAN

• *fitting control equipment and fuse boxes*

• *putting in wiring systems*

• *connecting wiring to sockets, light fittings and appliances*

• *testing wiring systems*

• *diagnosing problems and making repairs where necessary*

HANDY HINT
It's useful if you are able to work flexibly to fit in with customers' needs and be prepared to work in the evenings and on weekends. In some jobs you may be on call 24 hours a day in case of an emergency.

PLUMBERS

As a plumber, you carry out a wide range of tasks to install and maintain sanitation, heating and hot and cold water systems in all kinds of buildings. Your work may involve fitting the pipes for baths and toilets or laying drainage pipes. Some plumbers specialise in heating or air conditioning systems. If you work on gas systems, you'll fit and maintain gas appliances such as central heating boilers.

The work involves cutting, bending and joining pipes made from different materials, such as copper, aluminium and plastic. You use a variety of power and hand tools, such as cutters and welding equipment. As well as being practical and dexterous, you should also be able to follow technical drawings. It's important to be thorough too. Once the installation or repair is complete, you need to check that everything is working properly.

Plumbers regularly have to squeeze themselves into tight corners. This plumber is installing a new bathroom.

WHAT'S IN THE PIPELINE?

At times, you may have to work in uncomfortable, cold or dusty conditions. Dealing with blocked drains or toilets can be extremely smelly and unpleasant. You could be working all hours if you are on call for emergencies. If there's a gas or water leak, there's no time to lose. On the plus side, it is possible to become self-employed and earn a high salary. Well-qualified plumbers are always in demand.

HANDY HINT
Many people today are trying to save water in their homes and businesses. If you're thinking about becoming a plumber, it's worth finding out about green plumbing products such as water-efficient toilets and aerated water-saving shower heads, which use less water than ordinary models.

A plumber positions a pipe. Some plumbers work for building companies, but others are self-employed.

Ruthie – plumber

'After working for a year with a plumber, I took a two-year part-time course to learn all aspects of plumbing for water and heating systems and got my technical certificate. Then I started working as a self-employed plumber.

'I've been working for a few months and gaining experience. I've installed a bath-shower mixer tap, repaired leaky taps and replaced the ball valve in toilet cisterns. I've also helped another plumber to install a central heating system. This involved accurately measuring out piping and cutting it to fit.

'It can be a bit boring at first when you're a junior because sometimes there isn't much you're able to do – you just bring the tools and make lots of tea! It can be stressful while you're learning because if you make a mistake, such as causing a leak, you have to fix it with no extra pay.

'Once you're established though, plumbing is a reasonable business. People always need plumbers. Clients recommend you to their friends and then you get more work. It's a varied job too, with lots of problem solving. I find it very satisfying.

'If you're thinking about becoming a plumber, I'd say that if you're very handy and know something about plumbing already, you could go straight into a job. But if you don't have experience, I'd advise you to go to college first to become qualified.'

PLASTERERS

Plastering is another skilled interior job. Plasterers work on new and refurbished buildings, mixing and applying plaster on to surfaces so they are ready for decorating.

Most plasterers work on the solid plastering of walls and ceilings. In this job, you apply a base coat of plaster or cement, and then a fine coat of plaster over the top. Some plasterers fix plasterboards or metal wall linings to the walls to construct wall and ceiling partitions, although this is often carried out by specialists called dry liners. Dry lining is commonly used in modern buildings. Plastering work is mostly indoors, although you could also be applying rendering to outside walls.

TO BECOME A PLASTERER, YOU WILL NEED
●
to be physically fit
●
good manual skills
●
to work quickly
●
numeracy skills

FIBROUS PLASTERING
This specialist job involves making or repairing decorative plaster mouldings, such as ceiling roses or cornices. The plaster is reinforced with short lengths of fibre to hold it together. Some artistic ability is useful in this line of work.

Some general skills are useful for all plasterers. You'll require good co-ordination and numeracy skills to calculate the quantities of plaster needed. It's vital to be able to work quickly yet accurately – plaster dries fast!

A plasterer smoothes plaster over the ceiling in a new home. Plastering is a messy business – if they're working in an occupied building, plasterers must leave the workspace clean and tidy when they complete the job.

MAIN TASKS – INTERIOR PLASTERER

●

advising clients on suitable products

●

installing plasterboard

●

mixing plaster and applying it

●

sanding the finished plastering

●

clearing up after the job

WORKING CONDITIONS

Even if you're a plasterer working mostly indoors, it can be cold if the workplace is an unfinished building. You'll need to work up ladders and possibly on scaffolding, so a head for heights is helpful. Physical fitness is important too because you'll be on your feet or kneeling down for most of the day. Sometimes you'll need to wear protective gear, such as a helmet. As a plasterer, you'll move from site to site to work and may need to live away from home for some of the time.

ECO-FRIENDLY PLASTERING

As in all areas of construction, some people are seeking more eco-friendly ways of working. For example, new types of plaster have been developed that are made from natural materials and have insulating properties. They help to prevent heat loss through the walls in cold countries; in hot countries, they reduce heat gain. Keeping up with new technologies like these will help you to stay ahead of the game.

A specialist plastering job: these plasterers are restoring ornate plasterwork to its former beauty.

PAINTERS AND DECORATORS

Are you creative and skilful with your hands? If so, this job could be for you. As a painter and decorator you use paint or wallpaper to protect walls and ceilings and make them look attractive. You could be working in homes, institutions or factories.

You'll work with various tools, such as brushes and rollers. As well as having good manual skills, you need 'people' skills for liaising with clients, maths abilities for calculating the quantities of materials, and an appreciation of shape and colour.

Painting may sound fun, but remember that you will have to do a lot of work preparing the surfaces first. As in other interior jobs, you'll often find yourself working in awkward positions and up ladders. Yet it's a rewarding job too – you add the final touches to a building and see the job completed.

SPECIAL PAINT JOBS
Some painters and decorators have specialist jobs. They may undertake restoration work on old buildings, such as churches, to restore them to their traditional look. Others specialise in using eco-friendly paints, which do not contain substances that are harmful to the environment. They may also be safer for decorators who work with them and for the people who inhabit the building.

Decorators painting a room: one man uses a roller to cover large surfaces while his colleague uses a brush to ensure a neat finish around the vent.

WHERE WILL I BE?
It takes several years to become a qualified electrician, plumber, plasterer or decorator, whether you're learning purely on the job or studying part-time. Once you're experienced, you can decide whether to take the plunge and establish your own business. If you're successful, you can often make more money this way.

Simon – painter and decorator

'I've been a decorator and builder for 21 years. I found my first job at an employment centre – it involved painting and decorating a hotel. I didn't have any qualifications or experience but learnt on the job. During the early years of my career, I gained a qualification in hard landscaping, for building patios. Now I'm self-employed, and I mostly do painting and decorating work.

'I usually work from 8 a.m. to around 4.30 or 5 p.m., depending on the season and the amount of daylight. In the summer months, I can work longer hours. There's plenty of variety in this line of work. I could be high up on scaffolding, painting the exterior of a building, or indoors painting woodwork.

'I also enjoy meeting different people and seeing their satisfaction when I've finished, and the building looks greatly improved. The disadvantages are mostly to do with being self-employed, such as not having paid holiday leave. Sometimes the work is boring, if you're doing exactly the same kind of painting for a long time.

'I'd advise anyone who's interested in this job to find a suitable place to train. Doing an apprenticeship is ideal. Working on a large building site is great because it offers you opportunities to try out different kinds of work. Builders are amusing to work with too!'

This decorator is covering furniture and fittings before spraying paint to prevent any damage.

Technicians

Planning and organising a construction job is a major feat. Here's where the technical people come in – the site technicians, buyers, estimators and plant mechanics that make sure the project runs smoothly. If you're technically minded, there could be something here for you.

There are technicians for every stage of a construction job. For instance, if you're a roof technician, you're in charge of planning the construction of the roof. This includes estimating costs, scheduling and drafting plans and drawings. You'll liaise with everyone else in the roofing team. Once the job is underway, you'll survey the construction site and supervise the work.

As a technician, you may work in the site office or in a separate location, depending on the job. You'll mostly work a normal working week although sometimes there may be overtime when there's a rush to complete the project.

SITE TECHNICIAN

Site technicians help with the general running and safety of a building site. It's your job to make sure the right people are in the right place at the right time – with the correct equipment and materials. To do this job, you need to know about building materials and methods, and health and safety. It's essential to be a skilled organiser.

FINDING A JOB
To become a technician, it's useful to have taken science, maths and technology at school. You should also have some experience in an aspect of construction and knowledge of the whole building process. You'll need some training in technical drawing to understand the plans. You can start out as an assistant technician and train on the job, or take a job and study part-time, or go to college and get qualified first.

This technician uses special equipment to monitor air pollution at a building site.

A building site is inspected at every stage to ensure that the job is being carried out according to the specifications.

Anthony – site setting out engineer

'I've been training as a site setting out engineer for three years. I started without any experience, but am learning on the job. I work for a civil engineering company and attend college once a week to gain qualifications.

'I work in the site office for nine to ten hours a day. Most of my work involves setting out – ensuring the drawings are set out properly so the construction workers know the height, dimensions and position of the structure they're working on. I also write site diaries and keep progress records.

'The tasks vary depending on the job – there are different methods for each one. I've worked on a cliff stabilisation project and bridge construction. Recently we had to stabilise a railway line; there was a slope above and below it, and we had to prevent any movement of the line by laying down piles.

'The jobs are scattered around the country, so I usually have to work away from home from Monday to Friday. That's quite difficult, but I've become used to it.

'If you're considering a technical post, it's worth taking a job and studying at the same time. You have to spend much of your free time studying, but you'll learn fast and become qualified quickly.'

**TO BECOME
AN ESTIMATOR,
YOU WILL NEED**

●

numeracy skills for calculations

●

good computer skills

●

CAD experience

*Inspectors check the progress of
a project. The original estimates
for the budget and timescale for
a project sometimes prove
inaccurate and have to be revised.*

NUMBER CRUNCHING – ESTIMATORS AND BUYERS

If you have a head for figures, you could be an estimator or a
buyer. Estimators work out the total cost of the building job and
how long it will take. Buyers examine the design drawings to see
which materials and services are needed. They then purchase
everything that is needed for the project from building suppliers.
To do this, they contact suppliers to find the best prices and
arrange the delivery of materials when they're needed.

An estimator works out how much a building project will cost.
This includes building materials and the cost of labour and
equipment. Estimators need ICT skills to use accounting software.

COMPUTERS AND COMMUNICATIONS

For technician jobs, you'll probably be using computer-aided
design (CAD) to produce drawings, so excellent ICT skills are
essential. It's important to be an efficient organiser so that you
can work to deadlines. You'll require communications skills for
liaising with suppliers, site workers and managers.

MAIN TASKS – CAD OPERATIVE

●

discussing the brief with the team leader

●

working from existing drawings or models

●

using modelling software to make 2D and 3D drawings of a structure

●

using your designs to help prepare estimates of the project costs

A CAD operative works on the design for a chemical factory. If you'd prefer a desk job in the construction industry, this could be for you.

HANDY HINT

Working as a CAD operative might suit you if you'd prefer to work in an office in a quiet environment. You'll spend most of your time in front of a computer and will need to concentrate hard to produce accurate computer models.

CAD OPERATIVE

You can get a job purely working on CAD. This involves using computer software to create accurate drawings on screen to prepare a construction job. You could be working on the designs for houses, factories or bridges. It helps to have an interest in design and some knowledge of construction methods. For this role you'll be office based, working normal office hours, although you may be asked to do overtime at busy times.

At a junior level the job may be rather repetitive and routine – you could be working on drawings for small components or sections of a project. Once you're more senior, you'll have greater responsibility for the overall design of the project.

WHERE WILL I BE?
You can start out as a trainee technician and become a site technician. Then you could specialise in one area, such as buying or estimating. Alternatively, with further experience and degree-level study, you could progress to a professional-level job, for example, as a construction supervisor or manager.

PLANT MECHANIC

Enjoy fixing machines? You could be a plant mechanic. You'll need GCSEs in maths, technology and science as well as practical skills. Your job will include servicing, maintaining and repairing plant on site or in a workshop. If a machine breaks down, you'll be called in to diagnose the fault. Then you'll have to mend or replace the broken part and put the machine back together again. You'll test it to ensure it's safe for use.

You could be mending massive machines such as cranes, dump trucks, excavators or demolition equipment. You'll work on the engines and electronics as well as parts such as the wheels and tracks. For example, you might need to replace the digging arm of an excavator. You will use various kinds of power and hand tools, including cutting and welding equipment. Since most modern machines have electronic components, you'll be trained to use electronic equipment to check for faults.

WET, MUDDY AND COLD

You'll be working in all weather conditions on a dirty building site and perhaps even underground or at a great height. You'll need to be physically fit to cope with lifting equipment. Although you'll work a normal working week you may have to work overtime – machinery may be in use during the evenings or at weekends.

A paving machine is used for a road construction project. Plant mechanics play an important role in maintaining construction machinery.

Working as a plant mechanic can be a risky job. These workers high above the ground are assembling a crane.

Darren – plant mechanic

'I've been fixing machines for 21 years. First I took a job with a commercial garage and I studied part-time for two years to obtain qualifications as a mechanic. Eleven years ago I switched to fixing big plant.

'My job varies from day to day. I deal with breakdowns as well as routine service and maintenance. Tomorrow I'll be taking the track apart on a digger and putting on new seals to keep it tight. No two days are the same, so I never get bored.

'Sometimes I work extremely long hours. Construction workers need their machines up and running by the time they start work at 7 a.m. Recently I had to leave home at 4 a.m. to repair some dump trucks on site – exhausting! It's a satisfying job though. You might have eight machines backed up because of one broken one. You fix it, and people can get back to work.

'If you'd like to be a plant mechanic, I'd suggest becoming an apprentice for a dealership – a company specialising in one brand of machinery, such as JCB or Caterpillar. The company trains you to its specifications. Note that modern machines are computerised. You plug in your laptop to diagnose problems and check the fault code. So ICT skills are important. Finally, remember it's hazardous working with large machines and you must be conscious of health and safety at all times.'

Top Jobs

In the construction industry, you can work your way up to a senior management or professional job, for instance, as an architect or a civil engineer, surveyor or project manager. To achieve this, you need a degree or equivalent vocational qualification as well as relevant work experience.

**TO BECOME
AN ARCHITECT,
YOU WILL NEED**
●
to be creative
●
*excellent verbal
communication skills*
●
research skills
●
work experience
●
academic qualifications

ARCHITECT

Architects design new buildings and the space around them, and help to restore old buildings. They are involved with a construction project from start to finish. Architects have to consider how new buildings can be sustainable and need to follow developments in building technologies.

As an architect, your main tasks will include researching the sites that are to be developed, proposing designs to clients, producing technical drawings showing what the buildings will look like, and checking progress once the job is underway. You'll mostly be office-based but will make visits to the site – you'll certainly need to travel for work.

To become an architect, you have to study for several years and undertake training in an architect's office. You'll require ICT skills in order to use CAD in your work. It's important to enjoy drawing to make detailed designs, and you'll need first-class communication skills to present your ideas to your clients and encourage them to accept the plans! You'll need to be an excellent self-organiser to stick to deadlines.

An architect works on a scale model of a building. As well as being good at drawing, architects need to be able to work in 3D.

Architects make site visits to check that the building they have designed is going to plan.

Claire – architect

'I've been a chartered architect for 20 years. It took me seven years to qualify. I studied for a degree in architectural design and a post-graduate diploma in architecture, and took an exam to achieve chartered status. My training also included two years' work experience. For the last seven years, I've been running my own practice from home. My husband works for me, and when we're busy we take on temporary staff.

'In the mornings I meet clients, make site visits and have planning meetings, do some drawings and catch up with administrative tasks. I look after my children after school, and then start work again at 8 p.m. I continue with the drawing work, often until midnight. It's great helping people to design their dream home, and I love working from home and being my own boss.

'The hours are extremely long though and I never get away from work. Clients call me at any time, even at weekends. I also have to keep up with my professional obligations, such as attending professional development events.

'If you're thinking about becoming an architect, bear in mind that it takes a long time to qualify and that in times of economic recession, architects are some of the first professionals to lose their jobs. But it can be great fun and there are many opportunities to work abroad if you're adventurous.'

The construction of the Colorado River Bridge in the USA. When this five-year project is completed in 2010, the bridge will span the Black Canyon.

CIVIL ENGINEER

Whenever there's a big civil engineering project, such as a tunnel, wind farm, road or airport, civil engineers will be there to see the project through. They are involved from the beginning right through to its completion. Consulting engineers advise on the design of projects, while contracting engineers are involved throughout the construction process or help to maintain the structure once it is built.

Consulting engineers investigate the site for construction and prepare feasibility reports to check whether the plans are practical. They help to put together proposals and develop the designs, and may be responsible for approving the project drawings. Then they liaise with the contracting engineers to begin implementing the plans.

The contracting engineers schedule the work and supervise the project, dealing with the architects and building workers. They also communicate with the clients, keeping them updated on progress.

STRUCTURAL ENGINEER

Structural engineers play another important role in project design. Working alongside architects, structural engineers check how a building will stand up to the loads and stresses on it. They visit the site during construction to make sure the plans are being followed properly.

MAIN TASKS – STRUCTURAL ENGINEER

●

investigating ground conditions

●

calculating the loads and stresses on buildings

●

testing computer models to check the structure can withstand great forces, for example, strong winds

●

checking that the design is followed

Lucía – civil engineer

'I'm a qualified civil engineer and have been working in my current job for a construction company for ten years. I work in an office producing the plans for construction projects. This involves planning the mechanical installations (the heating, plumbing and fire precaution systems) and making the necessary calculations. I write reports that define how the installation will be carried out. I draw up plans, which are then passed on to the technical drawing team for completion.

'I work from 8 a.m. until 4 p.m. with a half-hour lunch break. My day is short because I have a young daughter. The others in my team work until 7 p.m. with an hour-and-a-half for lunch. Sometimes I have to bring work home to complete in the evening.

'We're particularly frantic during the last few days before a deadline when we need to deliver the project, and everyone has to put in long hours. Another downside is the pay; I don't feel I'm well paid considering the responsibilities I have. On the whole though, I enjoy the job because I'm always learning new things. I love going past a building knowing that I helped to design it.

'I'd definitely recommend becoming a civil engineer. It's hard work while you're at university but the main thing is not to get downhearted – your efforts will pay off in the end.'

Civil engineers and surveyors use instruments such as this theodolite to make precise measurements of angles for road and tunnel building, and other civil engineering projects.

SURVEYING THE SCENE

Surveyors analyse survey data so they can advise on the positioning of a new structure. It's the surveyors who make sure that bridges or pipework are located in the safest place possible.

As a surveyor, you could be responsible for surveying any kind of structure on land or water, either man-made or natural. On land, you could be a building surveyor, advising on all aspects of the design and maintenance of new and existing buildings. You might be a property surveyor, working for people who are buying, selling or developing properties. Alternatively, you could be working offshore as a marine surveyor. Maybe you'll be mapping the depth of the oceans to provide information for navigation or aiding the search for much-needed oil or gas resources.

Some surveying jobs are concerned with protecting the environment and using resources efficiently. For example, environmental surveyors advise on ways of minimising the negative effects of new structures on the environment. They look at ways of making existing buildings more energy efficient.

**TO BECOME
A SURVEYOR,
YOU WILL NEED**
●
*an interest in buildings,
landscape and
the environment*
●
good computer skills
●
excellent communication skills

Construction surveyors are responsible for overseeing construction projects. They use various types of technical equipment and computers.

Town planners work to improve transport systems. Here, concrete lining segments for the Channel Tunnel Rail Link are loaded on to a works train. This major construction project, completed in 2007, provided a high-speed rail link from London to the British end of the Channel Tunnel.

MAIN TASKS – TOWN PLANNER

●

using CAD or other IT systems to make models of the proposed development

●

analysing the effect of the development on a site

●

writing reports for local councils

●

presenting planning proposals at public meetings

●

negotiating between groups with opposing interests

MAKING PLANS

Just like surveying, many kinds of planning jobs exist. You could be planning anything from house extensions to major structures such as stations or bridges. Town planners work with local government to plan new urban developments, for example, shopping centres or sports facilities. They attend meetings with local government officers and local people to discuss the plans and consider the wider impact of the facility, including the transport options.

Town planners are involved in transport strategy in general. They have to work out how to cope with growing transportation requirements in cities often not built for large volumes of traffic. The planners may consider the improvement of rail and tram networks as well as roads.

Town planners often need to negotiate between groups with different interests. For instance, a local council may support plans to build a new airport to create jobs and expand economic opportunities in the region. However, environmental campaigners may oppose it because it will lead to an increase in carbon dioxide emissions. Emotions run high, and people become angry if the decision does not go their way. It's up to the planners to find a balance between the various interests.

A building developer and construction foreman examine the plans for a high-rise construction project.

MANAGING CONSTRUCTION

Construction projects involve large numbers of people and vast quantities of supplies. It's down to the management team to organise them all.

PROJECT MANAGERS

At the top level, the project manager has overall responsibility for a construction job – this could involve co-ordinating a massive project, such as building an Olympic stadium, with thousands of workers. As project manager, you're in charge of planning and managing the entire job, keeping to the schedule and the budget, and ensuring all the workers follow health and safety regulations. It's essential to understand legislation related to construction, such as building regulations and planning laws. You must also keep up with changes in the industry, such as new environmental protection laws, and ensure your company complies with them.

TO BECOME A PROJECT MANAGER, YOU WILL NEED

●

the ability to work under pressure

●

the ability to multi-task

●

leadership skills

●

proficiency in oral and written communication skills

WHERE WILL I BE?
You can enter the industry with a degree or equivalent qualification and join a training programme run by your employer to become a construction manager. Alternatively, you could work your way up from the technician level over several years, gaining experience in estimating, buying and site supervision and studying for a degree part-time.

CONSTRUCTION MANAGER

The next level down from project manager is the construction manager. In this role, you make sure work on site runs smoothly and deal with any problems. You are in charge of making sure all the materials are available at the right time – and within the budget. You organise the labour force so that you have the workers you need on site at the right time. You might be based in an on-site office or in a separate office. Wherever you work, you'll need to make regular site visits to check the project is going to plan. As well as a detailed knowledge of the construction industry, you'll need project management skills; ICT skills to run software packages to plan the workflow; numeracy skills to ensure you stick to the budget; and excellent communications skills to liaise with other professionals involved in the project.

FACILITIES MANAGER

This is the person who keeps a building well maintained once it's built. You'll employ people in the building trade such as electricians and plumbers to work for you as necessary.

The Olympic stadium building site in east London, under construction for the 2012 Olympics. The role of construction manager for a large-scale project like this is one of the top jobs in the industry.

MAIN TASKS – CONSTRUCTION MANAGER

●

checking the project plans with surveyors and architects

●

creating a schedule for the project

●

hiring people to do the work

●

organising the delivery of building supplies

●

checking progress and sorting out problems

●

liaising with the client

Further Information

BOOKS

Apel, Melanie **Careers in the Building and Construction Trades**, Rosen Publishing Group, 2005

Gisler, Margaret **Careers for Hard Hats and Other Construction Types**, McGraw-Hill Contemporary, 2008

Morton, Ralph **Construction UK: Introduction to the Industry**, WileyBlackwell, 2007

Pilgrim, Dee **Real Life Guides: Construction 2E**, Trotman Publishing, 2007

Reeves, Diane Lindsey, Gail Karlitz and Don Rauf **Career Ideas for Teens in Architecture and Construction**, Facts On File Inc., 2005

Senker, Cath **How to Get Ahead in Construction**, Raintree, 2007

Sumichrast, Michael **Opportunities in Building Construction Careers**, McGraw-Hill Contemporary, 2007

WEBSITES

http://careersadvice.direct.gov.uk/helpwithyourcareer/jobprofiles
Follow the link for construction industry job profiles.

www.careerstructure.com/Content/SoYouWantToBe.html
A guide to the technical, professional and managerial roles in construction.

www.bconstructive.co.uk
Information about construction careers and how to get a job.

www.careersinconstruction.com
A recruitment site with details of available jobs.

www.connexions-direct.com/jobs4u
Careers information for young people.

www.cskills.org
Information about training and working in construction.

Glossary

FURTHER INFORMATION / GLOSSARY

apprenticeship a training scheme that allows apprentices to work for money, learn a trade and become qualified

asphalt a mixture containing a black sticky substance called bitumen, used for making the surface of roads and for roofing

bituminous containing bitumen (*see* asphalt)

building regulations government rules to ensure that buildings are designed and constructed safely

ceiling rose the circular fitting on a ceiling used for attaching a light

chartered a measure of status which indicates that a person has reached the standard required to practise his or her profession at a high level

cladding a protective covering on a house made from a hard material

Computer-Aided Design (CAD) a software program that allows the user to create computer-generated drawings to prepare information for a construction project

conservation protection of a building of special architectural value

contractor a person or company that has a contract to do work for another company

cornice a decorative band of wood designed to hide curtain fixtures

damp-proof to place a material on walls or floors to repel moisture

dealership a business established to sell or distribute a company's goods or services in a particular area

dormer a vertical window made in the sloping roof of a house

dry lining attaching 'dry' plasterboard to walls and ceilings rather than a 'wet' plaster finish

emissions polluting waste products, such as carbon dioxide, that are released into the atmosphere

formwork temporary wood structures used to contain fresh concrete until it is strong enough to support itself

geothermal energy system a system using heat from underground, such as a heat pump

insulate to protect a building with a material that prevents heat from passing through

jigsaw a tool with a fine blade for cutting designs in pieces of metal or wood

joiner a person who makes the wooden parts of the building, such as doors

joist a long, thick piece of wood or metal used to support a floor or ceiling in a building

oxy-fuel cutting a process involving the use of gases and oxygen to cut metals

pile a type of foundation that is driven deep into the ground

plant heavy machines, such as cranes and diggers, used on building sites

plasterboard a building material made of sheets of cardboard with plaster between them, used for interior walls and ceilings

post-graduate diploma a qualification that you can take after a degree to prepare you for a particular job

rendering a layer of plaster or cement that is laid on a brick or stone wall to make it smooth

restoration repairing and cleaning an old building to make its condition as good as it was originally

roof sheeting a lightweight covering made from metal, plastic or a type of cement and attached to the roof

sander an electric tool with a rough surface used to make wood smooth

setting out transfer of information from a

designer's drawings to the situation on a building site

solar energy energy from the heat of the sun

spirit level a glass tube partly filled with liquid, with a bubble of air inside. It is used to test whether a surface is level; if the bubble is in the centre, then the surface is level.

subcontract to pay a person or company to do some of the work that you have been contracted to do

surveyor a person who examines a structure to check its condition or to examine or record the details of a piece of land or underwater structure

sustainable a building that is constructed and can be used with minimal resources so it creates little waste and does not harm people or the environment

telescopic forklift a forklift truck with a telescopic boom (long arm), which can lift heavier loads and has a longer range than other forklifts

thatching making a roof using dried straw or reeds

ventilating allowing fresh air to enter and move around a building

welding joining pieces of metal together by heating their edges and pressing them together

45

Index